WILD ON WHEELS

MOTORCYCLES THEN AND NOW

WILD ON WHEELS

MOTORCYCLES THEN AND NOW

Steve Otfinoski

BENCHMARK BOOKS

MARSHALL CAVENDISH
NEW YORK

Benchmark Books
Marshall Cavendish Corporation
99 White Plains Road
Tarrytown, New York 10591-9001

Library of Congress-in-Publication Data
Otfinoski, Steven.
Wild on wheels : motorcycles then and now / by Steve Otfinoski.
    p.   cm. — (Here we go!)
Includes index.
Summary: Describes how motorcycles and their use have changed over
the past hundred years.
ISBN 0-7614-0607-7 (lib. bdg.)
1. Motorcycles—Juvenile literature. [1. Motorcycles. 2. Motorcycle
racing.] I. Title II. Series: Here we go! (New York, N.Y.)
TL440.15.058   1998   629.227'5—dc21   97-3540   CIP   AC

Photo research by Matthew J. Dudley

Cover photo: *Image Bank,* G.M. Smith

The photographs in this book are used by permission and through the
courtesy of: *Ron Kimball:* 1, 14 (left and right), 15, 16, 17 (left and right),
back cover. *The Image Bank:* Michael Going, 2, 25; Patrick Curtet, 6-7,
11; John Banagan, 10 (top); Benn Mitchell, 10 (bottom); John P. Kelly,
12 (left); F.M. Whitney, 12 (right); Jay Silverman, 18-19; Terje Rakke, 20;
Alvis Upitis, 22 (left); Manfred Mothes, 22 (right), 26 (bottom), 27
(bottom); Melchior DiGiacomo, 23, 26 (top); Sobel/Klonsky, 27 (top);
Marc Romanelli, 30; Brett Froomer, 32. *Corbis-Bettmann:* 6, 9 (top).
UPI/Corbis-Bettmann: 8, 9 (bottom). *Photo Researchers, Inc.:* Richard
Phelps Frieman, 13 (top); Patrick Behar, 13 (bottom); Pat Boulland, 21;
Patrick Igoa, 24; Vandystadt, 28-29.

Printed in the United States of America

6 5 4 3 2 1

To Jamie and Jackie,
who are wild about things on wheels

Motorcycles have been zooming up city streets, around race tracks, and down dirt paths since German inventor Gottlieb Daimler first attached a motor to a bicycle back in 1885.

Motorcycles have always been exciting and, sometimes, dangerous. Daimler's teenage son was riding the first motorcycle when the seat caught fire. It was too close to the engine. Daring racers like Clarence Chamberlin (above) helped make motorcycles popular. In one race, he was thrown over a guardrail, got back on his motorcycle, and won the race.

By the 1920s ordinary people were riding motorcycles, like this very proper European couple. During World War II soldiers rode motorcycles in places a car couldn't go. Some cycles were equipped with machine guns. Others had sidecars for carrying the wounded to safety.

Today, all kinds of people enjoy riding motorcycles—
from adults in leather jackets to teenagers in T-shirts.
Riding alone or with a friend can be fun, but nothing
is as exciting as when cyclists from all over get
together at a road rally.

Not everyone rides motorcycles for fun. The man on the left commutes to work on his bike.
The police officer weaves in and out of traffic on his motorcycle to catch a speeding car or to get to the scene of an accident.

This street cleaner zips through the crowded streets of Paris on his rounds.

Daredevil stunt drivers leap over lines of cars and through rings of fire on their trusty machines. It's all part of a day's work for them!

There are many makes and styles of motorcycles to
fit the needs of every rider.
This Harley-Davidson (left) is made for cruising in comfort.
The Cafe racer (right) is a power machine, built for speed.
The classic 1946 Flathead (opposite page) has a
sidecar so you can bring a friend along for the ride.

Motorcyclists like their bikes to reflect their
personalities. They often will take a standard model
and customize it by painting it or adding new parts.
The Yamaha (opposite page) may be a Japanese bike,
but it's all-American now.

The owner of the big twin bike (above right) might
call his cycle a silver fox.

What would you name the customized bike on
the left?

Motorcycle racing is a thrilling sport. It's just you and your bike against a pack of other racers, speeding down a dusty dirt path or round and round a track. The winner is the most skillful rider with the fastest bike.

Motocross is the most popular kind of motorcycle racing. Kids as young as four years old can motocross, but whatever your age, be prepared for a rough ride. Cyclists race cross-country on a dirt track, splashing through water and mud. Hit a bump or go up a jump and you're suddenly airborne! If you take a spill, your helmet and padded clothing will protect you.
So climb on your bike and get back in the race!

Grand Prix means "big prize," and that's what the winner of this big-time race gets. Racers zoom on roadways or a track. At the starting line the racer "pops a wheelie" as he flies down the track. He puts on a burst of speed in the straightaway. As he rounds the final bend, the man at the finish line waves the checkered flag. The winner!

Circuit racing takes place on a specially made flat dirt track. The motorcycles are specially built, too—for speed and power.

A dragster is one of the fastest things on two wheels.
Some have two engines so they can go even faster.
Dragsters race in pairs on a quarter-mile straight track.
Some reach speeds of over 200 miles per hour.
The race is over in a few seconds. Blink and you
might miss it!

Two-person racing can be fun—with a sidecar or in the same machine.

This motorcycle looks more like a snowmobile.

Dune buggies are good for racing on sand dunes and other rough ground. That's where they got their name.

Spikes on tires help them grip the ice in ice racing. But they didn't help *this* racer much!

The motorcycles of tomorrow will be bigger and better—and safer. Antilock brakes will help riders stop their cycles in a skid. Plastic bodies will be more durable. Protective armor like that worn by this "knight rider" will prevent injuries. No matter how much they change, however, motorcycles will always make their riders feel wild on wheels.

INDEX

FIND OUT MORE

Armitage, Barry. *Motorcycles!* New York: Sterling Publications, 1988.

Barrett, Norman S. *Bicicross.* New York: Franklin Watts, 1990.

——————— . *Motorcycles.* New York: Franklin Watts, 1984.

Lafferty, Peter and David Jefferis. *Superbikes: The History of Motorcycles.* New York: Franklin Watts, 1990.

Lord, Trevor. *Amazing Bikes.* New York: Knopf, 1992.

Stewart, Gail. *Motorcycle Racing.* New York: Macmillan, 1988.

STEVE OTFINOSKI has written more than sixty books for children. He also has a theater company called *History Alive!* that performs plays for schools about people and events from the past. Steve lives in Stratford, Connecticut, with his wife and two children.